**This special edition book is present to you
with our best wishes and thanks**

**Our College is close to the historic town of
Harrogate featured in this book**

Queen Ethelburga's College

**Thorpe Underwood Estate,
York. YO26 9SS. England**

**Tel: + 44 1423 333 330 Fax: +44 1423 331 444
Email: info@QE.org Web: www.QE.org**

**The UK's Number 1 Top School for
Academic Results in the North of England.**

Girls & Boys 5 years to 20 years

PORTRAIT OF
HARROGATE

ANDY STANSFIELD

HALSGROVE

First published in Great Britain in 2009

British Library Cataloguing-in-Publication Data
A CIP record for this title is available from the British Library

ISBN 978 1 84114 876 2

HALSGROVE
Halsgrove House,
Ryelands Industrial Estate,
Bagley Road, Wellington, Somerset TA21 9PZ
Tel: 01823 653777   Fax: 01823 216796
email: sales@halsgrove.com

Part of the Halsgrove group of companies.
Information on all Halsgrove titles is available at: www.halsgrove.com

Printed and bound by Grafiche Flaminia, Italy

Introduction

The author comes from a parenthood which might have given rise to a War of the Roses: a mother from Newton Heath in Manchester, original home of Manchester United, and a father from the heart of the South Yorkshire coalfield. Early childhood brought about a natural inclination to fall on one side of the fence, almost literally, or the other and I chose my Mancunian heritage. Then some of my closest remaining relatives did the unthinkable: they moved to Yorkshire, introducing me to a hitherto unexplored part of the white rose county in the shape of Harrogate.

Harrogate surprised me, even then. It was softer, more genteel, less abrasive than the gruff coalfield towns I had previously perceived (in a typically biased Lancastrian way, of course) to be typically Yorkshire. I enjoyed walking its broad streets with their three and four storey residences which might be called merchants' houses in a south of England port. The Stray, Harrogate's enormous stretch of common land just off the town centre, seemed to go on forever and I remember being in awe of the Nidd Gorge running through neighbouring Knaresborough. Then relatives passed on and I moved on, not visiting Harrogate for many years until a period when work took me back once a year to a trade exhibition. Still living in Lancashire today, it is a pleasant one and a half hour drive through attractive countryside to Harrogate, making a possibility of a day out or a weekend with a night in one of the town's grand old hotels, not quite as grand as they used to be perhaps and thankfully their prices reflect that, but enjoyable all the same.

Although many first-time visitors have found themselves visiting this grand spa town to 'take the waters', these days more still visit to attend a trade show, exhibition or conference – a significant source of local income. The Royal Hall and Exhibition Halls lie at the foot of Parliament Street, opposite the old Royal Baths which now serve up sweet-smelling oriental cuisine rather than sulphurous fumes.

Nightlife has changed too. A late-evening stroll on a Saturday night sees the town centre transformed into a riot of rare gases, neon and helium to name but two, and a rarefied atmosphere due rather more to alcohol than spa water. But Harrogate's daytime is still presided over by Bettys Tea Rooms and the stately Montpellier Quarter. Thankfully, I must add. Gone is the rebel youth I once was.

The *piece de la resistance* is the town's Valley Gardens, first on the itinerary for the coachloads of visitors who alight around the corner at the bottom of Montpellier Hill. They not only provide an introduction to Bogs Field, site of 33 different mineral wells, but also the colonnade, sun pavilion and an audacious mix of plant species. It is even possible to continue one's walk through these world famous gardens out to Harlow Carr, the RHS garden on the western fringe of the town. Foliage and floral displays remain an important part of the town's visual impact.

The countryside around Harrogate, along with its towns and villages, are also worthy of exploration. Knaresborough and Ripley in particular will each offer great rewards for their inclusion in your plans, the latter having the most wonderful castle grounds just a short drive north from Harrogate itself.

Preparing this book over the course of several visits has rekindled some childhood memories it is true, but mostly it has provided me with fresh memories of previously undiscovered visual treasures and a desire to keep going back. No greater praise for a Yorkshire town could come from a passionate Lancastrian.

Andy Stansfield

Valley Gardens café
A popular venue winter or summer, the café in Valley Gardens is shaded by a wide variety of trees. Behind it lies a pool for model boat enthusiasts.

Bettys
The most famous place in Harrogate when it comes to sampling Yorkshire tea.

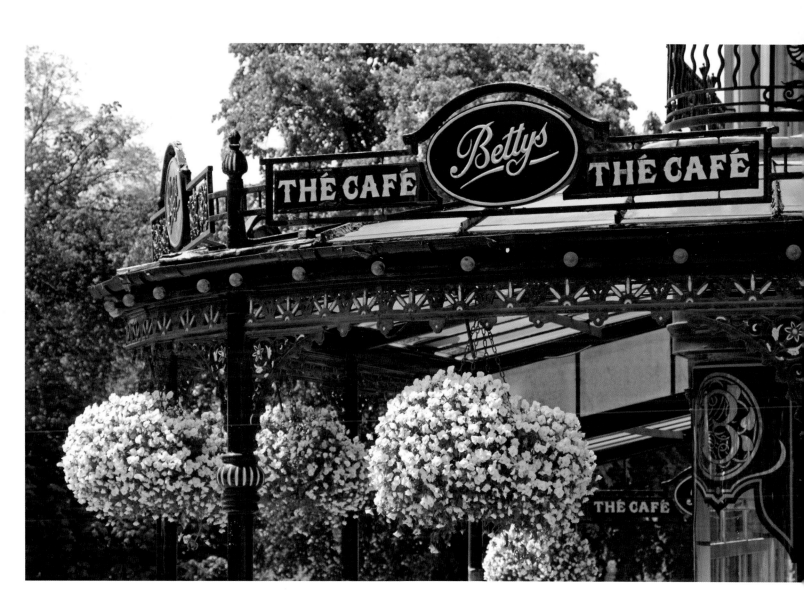

Spring flowers
Flower beds ablaze with colour in Valley Gardens.

Respite
No more than 20 yards into Valley Gardens, benches offer both respite for weary legs and a tranquil view.

Knaresborough Castle
The ruins and grounds
of Knaresborough Castle
are owned by
Her Majesty The Queen.

Nidd Gorge, Knaresborough
The River Nidd has carved its way through Knaresborough, creating spectacular cliffs which are forbidden ground for budding climbers.

11

Viewpoint
These statues perched on top
of the Victoria Shopping
Centre enjoy an unparalleled
view over Harrogate.

Bistro
The understated entrance to the Hotel du Vin & Bistro on West Park.

West Park
Elegant town houses fronted by colourful gardens line West Park, which leads towards The Stray from the war memorial.

Pastoral scene
Harrogate is surrounded by attractive rolling hills, seen here along the road to Otley.

Dangerous dip
A couple of miles west of Harrogate,
the A59 to Skipton has a notorious dip
which demands extra care from those
towing caravans and trailers.

Above: **Harlow Carr**
This Royal Horticultural Society garden is located on the fringes of Harrogate. If you fancy a double dose of flower power it is possible to walk through Valley Gardens, following the valley all the way to Harlow Carr.

Left: **RAF Menwith Hill**
Drivers approaching Harrogate on the A59 are treated to this unusual sight on their left. Basically a telecommunications listening operation, the base is owned by the RAF but run by the USA's National Security Agency.

Above: **Waterside**
Rowing boats can be hired along the River Nidd
at Waterside, Knaresborough.

Right: **Viaduct view**
Whether arriving by train across Knareborough's
famous viaduct, or looking up at the travellers
from below, this is undoubtedly the town's best view.

Underneath the arches
Images of Knaresborough's viaduct usually encompass the whole structure and its attractive setting. For once, here's a narrower view showing the attractive riverside cottages on the far side in more detail.

**Castle Mills,
Knaresborough**
View of the path along
Waterside with Castle Mills
on the left. This flax mill
dates from 1764 and
produced fine linen right up
until 1972, after which it was
converted into a number of
residences.

War memorial
At the top of the hill formed by Parliament Street lie the war memorial,
St Peter's Church, and both Cambridge and Prospect Crescents.

Prospect Crescent by night

Rape and poppies
This colourful scene was discovered along the valley of the River Crimple, which follows the treeline in the middle distance, on the eastern fringes of Harrogate.

Pennine scene
On the opposite, western, side of Harrogate the countryside has a more Pennine flavour, giving way to rock outcrops and heather-clad moors.

Catwalk Café
This small eatery on Montpellier Parade is highly recommended by the author.

Oriental eatery
Chinese restaurants can be found too, this one being on Station Parade opposite Library Gardens.

31

The Stray

Spring blossom brightens up The Stray, a large open area of common
land which once separated the original two villages of High and Low Harrogate.
In 1778 local residents were granted ". . . full and free ingress, egress
and regress in, upon and over the said 200 acres . . ."

24–26 James Street
University outfitters, Jack Wills, with its unusual window displays and canopy.

Busker
A saxophonist adds an atmospheric note or two to the James Street shopping experience.

35

The Crown Hotel

One of Harrogate's larger hotels lies just off the town centre at the foot of Montpellier Hill, convenient for both shopping trips and conferences. Lord Byron stayed here in 1806, during which visit he wrote the ode "To A Beautiful Quaker". The hotel was taken over by the Air Ministry in 1939 at the outbreak of World War II and it only reverted to its intended usage again in 1959.

Simply grand
Between Victoria Avenue and The Stray can be found this
grand terrace, set back from the traffic along West Park.

Swan Road

An interesting diversion which curves away from Royal Parade and the entrance to Valley Gardens, Swan Road contains the Mercer Art Gallery and several smaller hotels including Grants Hotel which is part of a terrace built for the Duchy of Lancaster in the 1880s.

THE RUINS AND GROUNDS OF
KNARESBOROUGH CASTLE ARE
THE PROPERTY OF HER MAJESTY
THE QUEEN IN RIGHT OF HER
DUCHY OF LANCASTER
THEY ARE LEASED TO THE
URBAN DISTRICT COUNCIL FOR
THE USE AND ENJOYMENT
OF THE INHABITANTS

Castle grounds, Knaresborough
This is a popular spot to sit and enjoy the views across the Nidd
Gorge and is just a two minute stroll from the centre of town.

Montpellier Gardens
This fascinating side street becomes The Ginnel as it draws nearer to Parliament Street. The Drum & Monkey pub can be seen on the right.

Windsor House
Overlooking Valley Gardens,
the towering edifice of
Windsor House and its
shapely roof can be seen
from all directions.

Hideaway
A solitary figure hides from the world and strong sunshine in this shelter in Valley Gardens.

Children at play
The central area of flowerbeds and lawns in Valley Gardens is the site of a number of mineral springs.
This feature depicting healthy looking children playing in water seems very appropriate.

Ripley
Only a short drive from Harrogate, Ripley is equally popular with visitors,
its castle and its ice cream being two of the main attractions.

Benches

Wherever you go in Harrogate, the park benches adopt the same elaborate snake-design for the supports. This one is on The Stray and the one below is by Montpellier Hill. They even use the same design in nearby Knaresborough.

Almscliff Crag
To the south-west of Harrogate this crag stands just outside the village of
North Rigton and forms the destination for a popular short walk.

Almscliff Crag
From the west the crag stands high above the fields below it, but this view from the south-east gives a better idea of the sedimentary nature of the rocks.

Floral art
Harrogate is very conscious of being home to one of the great UK flower shows and even its
roundabouts are works of floral art, like this one just off the town centre.

Spring blossom casts shadows over colourful bedding plants.

Cathcart House
Built shortly after 1860, Cathcart House
was a renowned boarding house on
West Park, counting Princess Alix of
Hesse, Empress Marie of Russia,
Queen Alexandra (Empress of India),
King Manuel of Spain, Prince Christopher
of Greece and Princess Victoria as visitors.

Window detail
Next door to Cathcart House stands West Park United Reformed Church, on the corner of Victoria Avenue and West Park.

Fewston
A view towards Fewston, from the Otley Road on the west side of Harrogate, with Swinsty Reservoir hidden by trees in the valley.

All Saints' Church, Kirkby Overblow
The attractive churchyard in the presumably windswept hilltop village of Kirkby Overblow, just south of Harrogate.

The Montpellier Quarter
Steps leading down to the bottom of Montpellier Hill.

Opposite: The gardens between Montpellier Hill and Montpellier Parade. There is also a Montpellier Road, Montpellier Street and Montpellier Gardens in the immediate vicinity.

The Royal Baths
Viewed from The Queen Mother's Rose Walk in Crescent Gardens,
the old Royal Baths are seen on the right.

Top: Today The Royal Baths serve as a restaurant.

Harrogate skylines at dusk
The Royal Baths.

Opposite: The Royal Pump Room.

Harrogate skylines by day
The rear of the Victoria Shopping Centre faces onto old chimney stacks and a new office block over the railway station.

Opposite: The same office block from Station Parade, with the 1887 Jubilee Memorial to Queen Victoria in the foreground.

Castle wall, Ripley
Wandering around the relaxing gardens of Ripley Castle, even its castellated boundary resembles
a walled garden rather than a form of fortification. In fact the gardens contain thousands of snowdrops,
bluebells, daffodils and narcissi as well as the National Hyacinth Collection.

Ripley Castle
This magnificent residence has been home to Sir Thomas Ingilby and his forebears for 700 years.
On the right of the picture, the Eel Tower used to contain an unroofed pond which was stocked
with freshwater eels, ensuring that this 'delicacy' was on the menu all year round.

Ripley Castle
The oldest part of the present structure, the gatehouse, dates back to 1450. A 75 minute guided tour details its fascinating history, while on the outside visitors are able to wander its extensive gardens throughout the year, apart from Christmas Day.

Ripley Castle
Archway detail.

Simulated history
Modern ornamentation, albeit
a reminder of the Tewit Well,
adorns the gardens in Station
Square with the Victoria
Shopping Centre beyond.

Promenade Square
This well-established horse chestnut provides shade for the houses lining Promenade Square.

Bonsai
This grower finds time to drive up from Nottingham to
sell his wares in the centre of Harrogate.

Opposite: Colonnade
This 600ft long colonnade in Valley Gardens provides a home
for a variety of climbing plants including roses and wisteria.

Blind Jack's, Knaresborough
Situated in the old centre of Knaresborough, this pub looks historic but was converted from two shops as recently as 1991. Nine pumps serve thirsty travellers with White Boar, Old Raby, Black Sheep and Timothy Taylor ales to name just a few.

Holy Trinity Church, Knaresborough
The spire of this Victorian church, situated on one of the town's older
streets called Briggate, peeks through the trees high above the River Nidd.

Any takers?
An unclaimed bench in Valley Gardens is an unusual sight. Just a short walk from the town's designated drop off/pick up point for coaches, Valley Gardens is often one of the first places coachloads of visitors head for.

Opposite: This is the norm, every bench occupied.

Above: **Bay Tree Cottage, Harewood**
A typical cottage frontage in one of the village's side streets.

Left: **Harewood village**
The majority of visitors to this village just outside
Harrogate head for Harewood House and its parkland setting,
but the village itself is attractive too.

Rambling rose, Valley Gardens
Climbing one of the colonnade's pillars, this rose caught the author's eye as it was lit by the sun, against the out of focus backdrop of different greens from a variety of tree species.

Tulips in Crescent Gardens
This bold display of tulips
was found in the gardens
opposite The Royal Hall.

Harrogate by night
The junction of Parliament Street and Crescent Road by The Royal Baths.

Opposite: A busy Saturday night along Parliament Street and a club named Rehab.

Above: **Family outing**
Rowing boats named *Jane*, *Jules* and *Polly* on the
River Nidd at Knaresborough.

Right: **River Nidd, Knaresborough**
Ducks are the only ones to take to the water, as all the
rowing boats remain moored to the quay at Waterside.

Follow the trail
The Floral Trail directs visitors around some of the more attractive sights of the town centre.

Crown Hotel
This crown-shaped plant holder forms part of the frontage of The Crown Hotel.

Montpellier Quarter
At the heart of this fascinating area just off Harrogate's town centre lies this jewellery shop.

Drum & Monkey
A short walk from the jeweller's lies this attractive corner pub.

The Old Swan Hotel
Situated on Swan Road, a stone's throw to the north-west of the town centre, this is one of a number of large hotels which serve those attending the many conferences and exhibitions put on by the town.

The White Hart Hotel
Personally recommended by the author, this hotel is also one of the most
convenient for Valley Gardens, the Montpellier Quarter and the town centre.

Jubilee Memorial
The foundation stone for this monument to Queen Victoria was laid in 1887 by the Mayoress, Mrs Ellis.

Library Gardens
A peaceful scene in the gardens which lie at the corner of Station Parade in the background and Victoria Avenue, adjacent to the Library.

Library Gardens
Modern art also makes Library Gardens an
interesting place to spend a quiet moment or two.

Montpellier Hill
Leading down from West Bank to the junction of Cold Bath Road and Royal Parade,
roadside parking is at a premium – as is the case all over Harrogate.

Montpellier Parade
With its flower beds, gardens, quaint lamp standards and sidewalk cafés, this is a popular spot for locals and tourists alike.

Royal Pump Room Museum
Crown Place, to the right of the photo, is marked by a plaque which details how the owner of the adjacent Crown Hotel tried to divert the public sulphur spring which fed The Royal Pump Room. A public outcry followed, along with prosecution for the hotel owner, Joseph Thackwray, in December 1835.

Royal Pump Room Museum
The Royal Pump Room, Harrogate's original sulphur well.

MG and bike
One of Harrogate's stylish benches is put to good use, providing a relaxed start to the day.

Closeness

This couple enjoy each other's company and the spring sunshine amidst the meandering pathways of the town's famous gardens.

The Montpellier by day

The Montpellier by night

Festival Pavilion by day
Originally constructed for the 1990 Gateshead Garden Festival, the Pavilion
was placed here in 1992. It contains a marble sculpture by Giovanni Maria Benzoni.

Festival Pavilion by night

Benzoni's sculpture *Cupid & Psyche* was purchased in 1862 by a Harrogate business syndicate and placed in the gardens of the Spa Room Estate. This area was then redeveloped in the fifties to build the Exhibition Halls and the statue was placed in storage and forgotten, until rediscovered in 1989 and relocated within this pavilion.

Shades of green
The huge diversity of greens in the Valley Gardens makes a picture in itself. In the
background can be seen the next generation of plants for distribution around the gardens.

Climbers
All along this 600ft colonnade climbers brighten up each of its brick pillars.

Whites
Appropriately named, this shop on West Park is typical of the former residences now used for commercial purposes.

West Park
The more grand residences are raised above ground level so as to provide a basement level too.

Above: **West Park**
The top of West Park, which leads to Parliament Street and the
town centre. Prince of Wales Mansions are on the right.

Left: **Prince of Wales Mansions and The Stray**
The huge expanse of grass, common land granted to the residents of
High and Low Harrogate before they became one, is broken up by bands
of spring colour. In the distance on the left of the picture stands
Prince of Wales Mansions, built in 1815. Originally a coaching inn
called Hattersley's, it was renamed The Brunswick in 1833, echoing
the name of Harrogate's first railway station which stood diagonally opposite.
In 1866 the name was changed to The Prince of Wales and in 1960 the
building was converted into prestigious apartments.

Shaded walks
This couple exercise their dogs along one of the
many tree-shaded paths across The Stray.

Opposite: Dappled shadows fall on another path across The Stray.

Estate villages
Ripley: the village was actually moved by half a mile to its present location early in the
Fourteenth century by the Ingilby family, owners of Ripley Castle for hundreds of years. Sir William Amcotts Ingilby
was the creator of the estate village you see today, most of it dating back to the 1820s.

Harewood: another village which owes much of its existence to a prominent local family and estate, in this case Harewood House.

The Tewit Well

Harrogate's spa status owes its existence to a variety of mineral springs and wells, the Tewit Well being the oldest. Located near the periphery of The Stray, the Tewit Well was discovered by William Slingsby in 1571. The present monument which today covers the well originally sheltered the sulphur spring in Low Harrogate until moved in 1842.

Opposite: the Tewit Well is easily accessed by a tree-lined path across The Stray.

Swan Road
Elegant town houses along Swan Road, on the north side of the town centre. Opposite lies Grants Hotel, part of a terrace originally built for the Duchy of Lancaster in the 1880s.

Retro office block
The Council Offices enjoy splendid accommodation with a view over The Queen Mother's Rose Walk.

Corner Farm
Most drivers heading for Harrogate from the west will speed past this attractive farm without a second glance, unless they happen to turn off onto the Otley road.

Beech Villa and Beech Lodge
These adjacent properties overlooking the Esplanade were built in the 1850s by the Duchy of Lancaster and served as private hotels. EM Forster stayed here in 1913 while writing one of his novels.

123

A secret revealed
This shelter overlooking the centre of Valley Gardens takes on the air of a secret revealed as it is glimpsed through the trees.

Sun Pavilion
This splendid construction with its glass domed roof is a popular venue for wedding receptions and other private functions.

Le Jardin Café and Bistro
Harrogate is not short of
places to to enjoy lunch or
dinner, this one being found
on Montpellier Parade
just below the famous
Bettys Tea Rooms.

Prospect Crescent
Sandwiched between
Cambridge Crescent and
Prospect Crescent, the latter
being in the foreground,
stands the town's war
memorial.

Windsor House
With a distinctive roof line, Windsor House can be picked out from much of the town centre once you've reached the top of Parliament Street as it dominates the the hill overlooking Valley Gardens.

Montpellier Baths

The plaque below the Montpellier Gardens street sign, with The Crown Hotel in the background, details the history of Montpellier Baths – originally The Crown Baths – which were once part of The Crown Hotel's estate. This small building was actually the ticket office which gave access to the sulphur spring which had a pump room built over it in 1822 by the hotel's owner.

Showpiece
The diminutive Festival Pavilion (left) and the entrance to the Exhibition Halls in the background.

The Royal Hall
Crescent Gardens with a colourful spring display of tulips and The Royal Hall in the background.

Above: **War memorial, Knaresborough**
Situated in the grounds of Knaresborough Castle, the war memorial stands
on the edge of the crags which tower vertically above the River Nidd.

Right: **Famous view**
This is perhaps Knaresborough's best known vista, taking in the
River Nidd and the railway viaduct, from the grounds of the castle.

Geometric planting
The carefully planned flowerbeds contrast with the multiple shades of green and variety of tree shapes in Valley Gardens.

Bogs Field

This area of Valley Gardens is known today as Bogs Field, and in the fifteenth century as Sauerkeld or Sour Springs. It is the location of 36 of Harrogate's 88 mineral wells and springs. These waters have never existed as rain and come from deep within the earth's crust.

Above: **Summer sunshine**
Local residents and visitors alike make the most of the June
sunshine, occasionally stopping to rest on some of the many
benches thoughtfully provided by the council.

Right: **Grand entrance**
A short walk from the official coach stop and entrance to
Valley Gardens is the start of their famous colonnade.

The Stray
Harrogate is well known for its extensive area of common land known as The Stray, only a few minutes' walk from the town centre.

THE STRAY

WHEN THE GREAT FOREST OF KNARESBOROUGH WAS ENCLOSED BY THE ACT OF 1770, AN AWARD DATING FROM 19TH AUGUST 1778 SET ASIDE AS COMMON LAND 200 ACRES BETWEEN THE ANCIENT VILLAGES OF HIGH AND LOW HARROGATE, TO PROTECT THE PUBLIC RIGHT OF ACCESS TO THE UNIQUE MINERAL SPRINGS AND TO PROVIDE EXERCISE SPACE FOR ALL IN SEARCH OF HEALTH. THE AWARD STATES '... THE 200 ACRES SHALL FOREVER HEREAFTER REMAIN OPEN AND UNENCLOSED, AND ALL PERSONS SHALL AND MAY HAVE FREE ACCESS AT ALL TIMES TO THE SAID SPRINGS ... AND ENJOY FULL AND FREE INGRESS, EGRESS AND REGRESS IN, UPON AND OVER THE SAID 200 ACRES...'. GRAZING RIGHTS WERE CONTROLLED BY GATEHOLDERS UNTIL THE 1893 STRAY ACT PASSED CONTROL TO HARROGATE CORPORATION, WHOSE SUCCESSORS ADMINISTER, BUT DO NOT OWN, THIS PRICELESS PUBLIC ASSET.

HARROGATE BOROUGH COUNCIL 1925

Crown Place
Next to The Royal Pump Room Museum, customers of The Crown Hotel's bistro can enjoy a drink outside in historic surroundings.

James Street
Hoopers department store is just one of several attractive shops along colourful James Street.

Tropical Harrogate
The luxurious growth of these plants along the stream running through Valley Gardens is extraordinary.

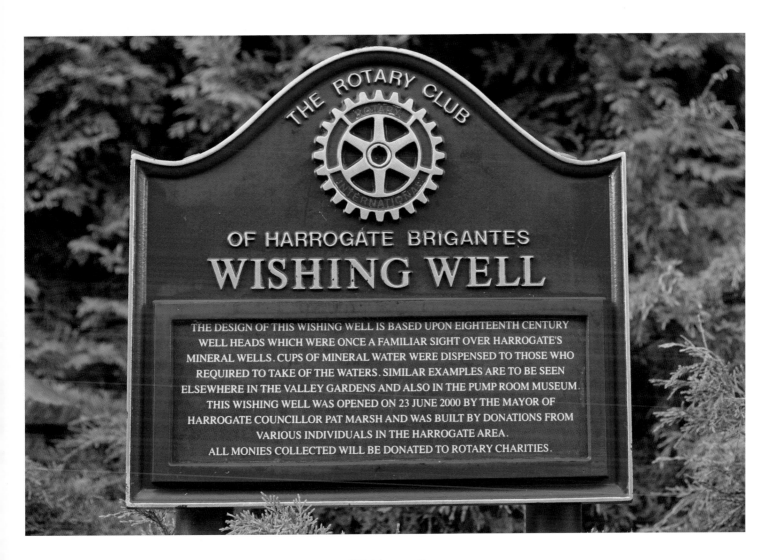

THE ROTARY CLUB

ROTARY INTERNATIONAL

OF HARROGATE BRIGANTES

WISHING WELL

THE DESIGN OF THIS WISHING WELL IS BASED UPON EIGHTEENTH CENTURY WELL HEADS WHICH WERE ONCE A FAMILIAR SIGHT OVER HARROGATE'S MINERAL WELLS. CUPS OF MINERAL WATER WERE DISPENSED TO THOSE WHO REQUIRED TO TAKE OF THE WATERS. SIMILAR EXAMPLES ARE TO BE SEEN ELSEWHERE IN THE VALLEY GARDENS AND ALSO IN THE PUMP ROOM MUSEUM. THIS WISHING WELL WAS OPENED ON 23 JUNE 2000 BY THE MAYOR OF HARROGATE COUNCILLOR PAT MARSH AND WAS BUILT BY DONATIONS FROM VARIOUS INDIVIDUALS IN THE HARROGATE AREA. ALL MONIES COLLECTED WILL BE DONATED TO ROTARY CHARITIES.

Wishing well
This unusual feature harks back to the days when the town's curative waters were dispensed by the cupful.

Station Square gardens
One of many restful locations around the town where it is possible to sit with a book or newspaper and watch the world go by.